SYMBOLS OF THE SEASON:

Exciting Epiphany Experiences

Phyllis Vos Wezeman

Jude Dennis Fournier

DEDICATION

To Herm and Gayle Schutt...
...With appreciation for the ways in which the light
of God's love shines through your gift of friendship.
(PVW)

To my godchildren...
Kimberly Ann Smith
Kara Kay Fournier
Matthew John Toporski
...whose lives have been a gift to me.
(JDF)

SYMBOLS OF THE SEASON:
Exciting Epiphany Experiences

*by Phyllis Vos Wezeman
and Jude Dennis Fournier*

Copyright © 1991
EDUCATIONAL MINISTRIES, INC.

Printed in the United States of America. All rights reserved. No portion of this book may be reproduced by any means without the prior permission of the copyright owner.

ISBN 1-877871-26-5

EDUCATIONAL MINISTRIES, INC.
165 Plaza Drive
Prescott, AZ 86303-5549

TABLE OF CONTENTS

INTRODUCTION 5

SEEKING THE SAVIOR: CROWN 7
    Overview 8
    Crown Cloths 9
    Royal Runner 11
    Crown Cake 12
    King-Size Kings 13
    Majestic Music 15
    Shared Stories 16

SIGN OF THE SAVIOR: STAR 17
    Overview 18
    Kingly Kaleidoscopes 19
    Singing About Stars 21
    Shining Stars 24
    Glow-in-the-dark Galaxy 26
    Scripture Stars 28
    Faithful Followers 30

SEARCHING FOR THE SAVIOR: PATH 33
    Overview 34
    Seeker's Story 35
    Diorama Display 37
    Scripture Search 39
    Personal Paths 40
    Faith-Filled Followers 42
    Syncopated Story 43

SYMBOLS OF THE SAVIOR: GIFTS **45**
    Overview 46
    Clothing Collection 47
    Purposeful Poetry 49
    Great Gifts 51
    Tangible Treasures 52
    Tree Trimming 54
    Reflective Responses 55

SURRENDER TO THE SAVIOR: HANDS **57**
    Overview 58
    Prayerful Procession 59
    Creating With Clay 61
    Meditative Moments 62
    Special Symbols 64
    Litany Of Light 66
    Signing A Song 68

SERVING THROUGH THE SAVIOR: WORLD **71**
    Overview 72
    Patchwork Pieces 73
    New Narratives 75
    Projecting People 77
    World Walk 78
    Singing Songs 80
    Participatory Prayers 81

INTRODUCTION

In some religious traditions, Epiphany, January 6, is observed for one Sunday as the day on which Christians celebrate the visit of the Magi to the Christ child. In others, it is considered a season of the church year and may include as few as four or as many as nine Sundays, depending on the variable dates of Lent and Easter. These Sundays during or after Epiphany give witness to the ministry and mission of Jesus. They begin with the baptism of the Lord, include his first miracle at the wedding at Cana, and end with the transfiguration. The Scripture stories focus on Jesus' teachings, his calling of disciples and his mighty acts which testify to God's saving presence among His people.

The word Epiphany comes from the Greek word "epiphaneia" which means appearance, manifestation or a showing forth. Jesus' identity and divinity were revealed through the visit, worship and gifts of the Magi, his baptism and his first miracle. In the words of an ancient Roman prayer, "Today you revealed in Christ your eternal plan of salvation and showed him as the light of all peoples. Now that his glory has shown among us you have renewed humanity in his immortal image."[1]

Symbols Of The Season: Exciting Epiphany Experiences is a book which focuses on Matthew 2:1-12. Through six themes found in this Scripture passage, and symbols which represent them, it explores the significant story of the visit of the Magi to the Christ Child. Six learning activities for each theme and symbol are designed to help participants experience, understand and appreciate the events in creative, concrete and challenging ways.

The six themes and their symbols are:
- Seeking The Savior: Crown
- Sign Of The Savior: Star
- Searching For The Savior: Path
- Symbols Of The Savior: Gifts
- Surrender To the Savior: Hands
- Serving Through The Savior: World

The activities in this book may be combined to form lessons for church school classes as well as employed as supplements to existing curriculum. The 36 experiences can be used to enhance worship, education and outreach events. Families and day schools will find the ideas valuable for Epiphany celebrations, too.

---

[1] Simcoe, Mary Ann, Editor. Christmas Sourcebook, A. Chicago: Liturgy Training Publications, 1984, p. 105.

SEEKING THE SAVIOR

SYMBOL: CROWN

OVERVIEW

Matthew 2:1-12 is a story about kings: three or more scholarly kings called Magi, a subversive king known as Herod, and the supreme king of heaven and earth named Jesus.

Magi, from the original word "magoi," is the title that was given to philosophers, priests or astronomers in the region of Persia. These Wise Men served as teachers and instructors of the Eastern Kings. People sometimes called the Magi kings, and considered them to be important counselors, soothsayers and interpreters of dreams. "These trained astrologers with the insatiable curiosity characteristic of scientists had seen a remarkable astrological phenomenon, the exact nature of which is not disclosed; and, being familiar with the current widespread belief that the time was ripe for the appearance of a king to be born in Judaea who would claim universal homage and usher in a reign of peace, they set out for that country to test the truth of their conjecture."[2] The number of Wise Men who journeyed to find Christ is uncertain. Because three gifts were offered to the child, three is the number of Wise Men associated with the story. Legend has given the kings the names Melchior, Gaspar and Balthasar.

King Herod, the Roman ruler of the region at the time of Jesus' birth was an evil tyrant. "He was afraid that this little child would interfere with his life, his place, his power and his influence."[3] The ruthless ruler asked the wise men the time and place of the birth of the baby and proceeded to make plans, both publicly and privately, to destroy the new rival.

At the time of Jesus' birth, the Jews were anxiously awaiting the Messiah. They supposed that he would be an earthly king who would deliver them from Roman rule. Jesus, a descendent of Israel's greatest king, David, was born the King of the Jews. As king of heaven and earth, he ruled as a shepherd tends his flock, both tenderly and faithfully.

The symbol generally associated with a king is a crown, and the six activities in the section "Seeking The Savior" all involve the use of a crown. The experiences are intended to help the participants review and remember the stories of the Wise Men and of Herod, but more importantly, to respond to the story of the Savior.

---

[2] Tasker, R. V. G. <u>The Gospel According To St. Matthew: An Introduction And Commentary</u>. Grand Rapids, MI: Eerdmans, 1968, p. 37.

[3] Barclay, William. <u>The Gospel Of Matthew, Volume 1</u>. Philadelphia: Westminster Press, 1975, p. 30.

CROWN CLOTHS

PURPOSE

To make a banner symbolizing the different types of kings represented in the Epiphany story.

PREPARATION

- Cut crown patterns
- Prepare a burlap background for each individual, or make one banner for the class to use.

You will need the following materials for this activity:
- Cardboard
- Crown patterns (page 10)
- Burlap, natural colored
- Felt, various colors including dark blue, purple, red, gold and brown
- Glue
- Scissors
- Pencils
- Dowel rods
- Yarn or twine
- Puff paint
- Bible

PROCEDURE

Create individual or group banners and represent each of the kings mentioned in the Epiphany story with a different type of crown.

Start by asking the children to name the kings cited in the story. Their answers should include the Magi, Herod and Jesus. Ask what type of crown might symbolize each of these kings. The Magi probably wore turbans or jewel studded crowns. Herod's headpiece could suggest the greed and evil depicted by his personality. Jesus wore a crown of thorns. Read Matthew 27:29 to the group. It mentions this unique crown.

If each child is to make a personal banner, pass out crown patterns, pencils, felt and scissors. Instruct the group to trace and cut a crown shape for each king. Encourage the use of dark blue, purple and gold for the crowns of the Wise Men, red to represent Herod, and brown for the crown of thorns worn by Jesus. When the cutting is completed, distribute a burlap banner background to each person. Place glue within reach of all participants. Guide the group as they glue the crowns to the fabric. Center the crown of thorns on the banner and arrange the other crowns around it. The Magi's crowns and Herod's crown might even touch Jesus' crown in some way.

Additional symbols and decorations may be placed on the banners. Some ideas are to glue a felt star near the crowns of the Wise Men. Encircle gold coins through Herod's crown to symbolize greed. Puff paint, used according to package directions, provides another way to add dimension and detail to the banner pieces. Suggest drawing faces on the coins or designing light rays reaching from the stars.

Once the banners are completed, give each learner a dowel rod and help him or her slip it through the casing at the top of the banner. Pass each person a length of yarn or string to serve as the hanger for the banner. Assist the children as they tie one end of the yarn to each side of the dowel rod.

Use the individual banners to decorate the classroom, attach them to doors throughout the building, or ask the children to hang them on the front doors of their homes.

One large banner could be made by the entire class. It would be a beautiful addition to a procession for a worship service.

CROWN PATTERNS

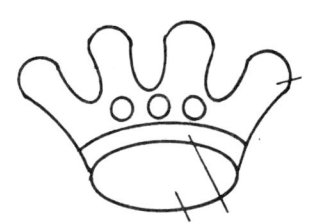

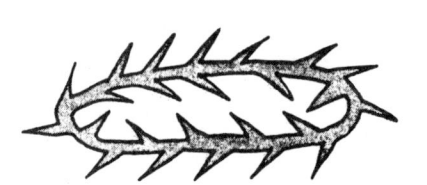

ROYAL RUNNER

PURPOSE

To tie-dye a piece of cloth with colors that will suggest the royalty and majesty of the Magi and of the infant they sought.

PREPARATION

You will need the following materials for this activity:
- Liquid dye; dark blue, shades of purple, red
- Rubberbands, thick
- Twine or heavy string
- Coffee cans, large
- Rubber gloves
- Fabric, white cotton or pieces of bed sheets

PROCEDURE

Remind the children that the Wise Men came to worship the King of Kings. Cut white fabric to the desired length and width. Wind the length of the fabric tightly, fold it in half and wind it again in a braid fashion. Hold the braid in place with many rubber bands or heavy cord.

Prepare liquid dye according to package directions. Use a different coffee can to mix each color. Any left over dye can be saved in the cans and used again. Dip one end of the braid into a dye bath and hold it in the solution for several minutes. Using rubber gloves, remove the cloth from the dye and ring it out. Dip the opposite end of the fabric into another color. Remove the piece and ring it tightly. Remove the rubberbands or twine. Open the cloth and allow the runner to dry. To add more color, begin the procedure again using more rubber bands and different color dyes.

Use the completed piece as a table runner in a worship center for the sanctuary, classroom or home. Share the beauty of the runner by using it on a prayer table during an Epiphany worship service or display it in a home as part of the decorations for the Epiphany season.

The same procedure may be used to create costumes for an Epiphany pageant, or to make stoles for clergy, teachers or children to wear during the reading of the Epiphany Scripture passage.

Crown Cake

PURPOSE

To make a cake depicting a crown which might have been worn by a king who sought the Savior.

PREPARATION

You will need the following materials for this activity:

For cake: 1 1/4 cups margarine, softened, 2 3/4 cups sugar, 5 eggs, 1 tablespoon freshly squeezed lemon juice, 3 cups flour, 1 teaspoon baking powder, 1/4 teaspoon salt, 1 cup evaporated milk, 2 teaspoons grated lemon peel.

For glaze: 1/3 cup margarine, softened, 2 cups powdered sugar, 2 - 3 tablespoons freshly squeezed lemon juice, Hot water.

Also: Candy gum drops, Mixer, Bowls, Baking equipment, Tube pan, Oven, Knife, Plates, Forks, Napkins, Cups, Juice.

PROCEDURE

Explain to the participants that they will be making a cake symbolizing a crown which might have been worn by one of the Wise Men. Invite them to measure and mix ingredients, and to share in the results.
Heat the oven to 350 degrees.
Combine margarine, sugar, eggs and lemon juice in a large mixer bowl on low speed for one minute, scraping the bowl constantly. Beat five minutes on high speed. Mix in flour, baking powder, and salt alternately with milk on low speed. Add lemon peel.
Pour the batter into a greased and floured tube pan. Bake for one hour and 15 minutes. Cool the cake in the pan for 20 minutes. Remove it from the pan and allow it to cool.
Make the glaze by melting one-third cup margarine, and stirring in two cups powdered sugar and the lemon juice. Beat until smooth. Add one tablespoon of hot water at a time until the mixture reaches the desired consistency. Pour over the cake.
Decorate the cake with candy gum drops of various colors and sizes to represent jewels.
Share the cake with the participants, or make several cakes and serve them at an all-church event or Epiphany party.

KING-SIZE KINGS

PURPOSE

To create giant puppets, representing the Wise Men, to use at an Epiphany event.

PREPARATION

You will need the following materials for this activity:
- Paper
- Pencils
- Aluminum clothesline poles
- Bleach bottles, large (Be sure to clean the bottles and remove the labels. Allow the bottles to dry.)
- Hangers
- Duct tape
- Pantyhose (old ones which have been washed)
- Paper towel tubes
- Packing material (thin styrofoam-like material used for packing)
- Cardboard
- Scissors
- Felt
- Tacky glue
- Fabric
- Plastic bags, various colors
- Trims
- Yarn
- Dowel rods, optional

PROCEDURE

Giant puppets, created primarily from recyclable materials, can be an attractive and attention-getting addition to Epiphany education events, worship services, and special parades and programs. The puppets can be made by individuals, classes or groups. A variety of characters, including the Wise Men, are possible.

Provide information on the Magi and have each child or group choose one for which they will make a puppet person. It may be helpful to distribute paper and pencils and suggest that a sketch of the puppet be made before the actual work begins.

Distribute the bottles, which will become the puppet's head. Tell the children to turn their bottles upside down and to decide if the handle will be used on the front of the face as the nose, or if it will be turned to the back and not seen.

Pass out the aluminum clothesline poles. The pole is the puppet body. Also give each person a hanger and tell him or her to straighten the hook. Instruct the children to insert their pole into the opening of their bottle. Next, direct them to insert the straightened portion of the hanger into the bottle opening on the front side of the pole. Provide duct tape and have each person wrap it around the pole, hanger and bottle to fasten them together.

Cut legs from pantyhose and give one to each person to pull over his or her bottle to form the skin. Try to give the children a choice of color to correspond to the skin tones of their "people." Have them gather the pantyhose around the neck, trim the excess and tape it to the pole.

Make felt scraps available and ask the learners to cut facial features, such as eyes, nose, mouth, eyebrows, eyelashes and cheeks, and to glue them in place. Be sure the pieces are large enough, even over-sized, to be seen from a distance.

The arms are formed from a full pair of pantyhose and four paper towel tubes. Demonstrate how to do this and then allow time for the children to complete the procedure. Insert a tube into a pantyhose leg and knot off. Insert the second tube and knot again. Repeat the procedure for the other leg. Pull the pantyhose up over the hanger. Gather and tape it around the neck. Allow the arms to hang from the sides of the hanger. If legs are desired, they may be formed in the same way. Attach them to the center of the puppet body.

Show the young people how to pad the body and to provide an underlining for the costume by wrapping strips of sheets of packing material around the bodice. If the costume is to have a skirt, gather packing material around the waist to provide fullness. Help the children do this part. They may need to work in pairs so one person can hold a pole while the other one tapes the packing in place. Recycled plastic bags, available in a variety of designs and colors, may be used for the costume. Fabric, if employed, should be lightweight so it doesn't make the puppet too heavy when carried. Packing material, which can be spray painted, may also be utilized. Split the plastic bags at the sides and extend them to their total length. Use them, as well as pieces which have been taped together, to form shirts, blouses, vests, skirts, pants and any other items of clothing. Trim with different textures and materials to create the desired effect.

Pass out cardboard and have each child trace two hands, theirs or a partner's, and cut them out. Poke a hole into the top of each hand, give lengths of yarn, if needed, and tell the children to attach one hand to the bottom of each arm.

Guide the children in making hair from yarn, polyester stuffing, fake fur or plastic bags, and attaching it to the top of the puppet's head.

To allow for movement and gestures, give each child a dowel rod to attach to one of the hands.

Tell the youngsters to use the aluminum pole as the rod to carry the puppet. It may be carried by one person and a second person may work the arm.

Use the king-size kings in a drama during the church school hour, a processional for a worship service, or as part of a program or parade for an intergenerational Epiphany celebration.

MAJESTIC MUSIC

PURPOSE

To help the children experience the story of the Savior King through majestic music and personal paintings.

PREPARATION

You will need the following materials for this activity:
- Watercolor paper, 12" x 14" (cut into large crown shapes)
- Water color paints, various colors
- Brushes, several sizes
- Cups
- Water
- Record or tape of the "Hallelujah Chorus"
- Record or tape player

PROCEDURE

Invite the young people to listen to music which describes Jesus as the King of Kings. Play the "Hallelujah Chorus" from The Messiah. After the children have heard the selection once or twice, provide supplies so that they may paint a crown to represent the majesty and glory of the Savior the Wise Men sought.

Place cups of water, paint trays and brushes on the tables. Pass out a paper crown to each person. Tell the children that the music will be played again. Invite them to respond to the music by painting the crown. Additional music may be played during the activity.

Turn the music paintings into Epiphany greeting cards and send them to people who live out of town. Miniature crown paintings can be made as tree decorations.

SHARED STORIES

PURPOSE

To read books, listen to tapes, and watch videos which illustrate the story of the Wise Men and to compare and contrast the presentations.

PREPARATION

You will need the following materials for this activity:
- Books
- Cassette tapes
- Cassette tape player
- Videos
- Video equipment
- Bible story books

PROCEDURE

The story of the Wise Men, found in Matthew 2:1-12, is available in many formats. Tell it to the children using books, tapes and videos. Try some of these materials:

Books:
The Visit Of The Wise Men. St. Louis, MO: Concordia. An "Arch Book" which retells the story of the journey and visit of the Wise Men.

The Story Of The Other Wise Man. Henry Van Dyke. New York: Ballantine Books, 1984. A cherished tale of the power of love.

Bright Star, Bright Star, What Do You See? Maxwell, Cassandre. Nashville: Cokesbury, N.D.

Cassette:
"The Visit Of The Wise Men." Arch Book/Tape Series. St. Louis, MO: Concordia, N.D. An audio cassette of the story of the Magi's search for the Savior.

Video:
"The Other Wise Man." Ft. Worth, TX: Brownlow, N.D. Touching story of Artaban, the fourth wise man, who sold all he possessed and bought three jewels to present to the Christ child.

Compare and contrast the ways in which the story of the Wise Men is presented in the various formats. Provide a collection of Bible story books for the participants to read too.

SIGN OF THE SAVIOR

SYMBOL: STAR

OVERVIEW

"Centuries ago, in the ancient East, the study of the stars was for some the gateway of religion. In the movement of the constellations, in the conjunctions of the planets and other signs which were observed in the skies, the astrologers and other followers believed that they could read the thoughts of God in the stars. Wise Men from the East were probably out of this background. They could have held to the beliefs that the heavenly bodies influenced the lives of human beings and that through a complex scheme of determining the movements of those bodies, the future could be known. An unusual arrangement of the heavenly bodies would indicate some special event. The Magi were most likely familiar with the ancient prophecies, such as Number 24:17, concerning the coming of a King, whose birth was to be preceded by a sign in the sky."[4]

Although the exact nature of the star which led the Magi is unknown, there are many theories about it. The most probable is that near the time of Jesus' birth, there was a brilliant conjunction of the planets Saturn and Jupiter. It is also possible that the bright light was a comet seen in the atmosphere rather than in the heavens. Since it was the Wise Men's profession to watch the skies, some heavenly brilliance spoke to them of the entry of a great King into the world. It initiated their search to seek him and to pay him homage.

Six activities in the section "Sign Of The Savior: Star" use a variety of creative methods to help the participants experience the Scripture story of the star which led the Wise Men to find Jesus. The lessons are also designed to encourage the children to explore ways in which they seek and find Jesus in their daily lives.

---

[4] Schneider, Kent and Sr. Adelaide Ortegel, S.P. The Burst Of Christmas: Alternative Christmas Celebrations. West Lafayette, IN: Center For Contemporary Celebration, 1975, p. 33. Used with permission.

KINGLY KALEIDOSCOPES

PURPOSE

To make a kaleidoscope and to use it to discover the awe and wonder associated with the Wise Men's experiences.

PREPARATION

You will need the following materials for this activity:
- Beads, small
- Sequins, various colors
- Confetti
- Paper towel tubes
- Cellophane wrap, white and yellow
- Masking tape
- Wrapping paper, various patterns
- Glue
- Scissors
- Pencils

PROCEDURE

The wise travelers looked to the stars and found the awe and the wonder of surprise. One star shown brighter than all the rest. Its tail streamed down to earth and filled the sky with color, beauty and mystery. Each person's life is full of beauty and surprise. People look in all directions to seek out wonder and awe. It is found in the Infant Child, the person of Jesus. This fun kaleidoscope project will encourage the children to discover some of the awe and wonder the Wise Men must have experienced as they sought and found the Savior.

Demonstrate the method for making the kaleidoscope before distributing the materials to the participants.

Cut a two inch piece off of one end of a paper towel tube. Wrap yellow cellophane over one end of the small piece and tape it in place. This will become the bottom of the instrument. Place small colored beads, sequins and confetti inside of the two inch section. Wrap and tape clear cellophane over the top of the small piece of tubing.

Tape the top of the two inch piece of tube to the bottom of the large tube. Cover the top of the kaleidoscope with several layers of masking tape so that the top end is completely covered with a heavy thickness of tape. Insert a pencil into the center of the masking tape to form a peep hole.

Wrap the sides of the kaleidoscope in bright, colorful paper. Do not cover the bottom or the top.

Provide supplies and assist each person in the class as he or she creates a kaleidoscope. When the project is completed, allow time for the children to look through their kaleidoscopes and to discover the awe and beauty of the various shapes and designs that are formed. Tell the participants to move their kaleidoscopes from side to side and to rotate them so that many patterns and scenes can be created.

SINGING ABOUT STARS

PURPOSE

To sing songs to reinforce the story of the star which led the Wise Men to the Christ child.

PREPARATION

You will need the following materials for this activity:
- Music
- Piano, organ or guitar

Locate a variety of hymnals and songbooks which contain Epiphany music. Ask an accompanist to play during the singing.

PROCEDURE

Traditional hymns, as well as new music, about the star which led the Kings to the Christ child, are contained in hymnals and songbooks. Try singing some of them. The book in which the song is contained is listed first, and the specific titles are included below it. The page number on which the song can be found is in parentheses after the title.

Avery And Marsh Songbook, The. Avery, Richard and Donald Marsh. Carol Stream, IL: Agape, 1972.
- Shine, Star! (52)
- Starlight (59)
- Take Time (23)
- Will Any Three Leaders (49)

Everflowing Steams: Songs For Worship. Duck, Ruth and Michael G. Bausch. New York: Pilgrim Press, 1989.
- Arise, Your Light Has Come (32)
- I Am The Light Of The World (33)

New Hymns For The Lectionary To Glorify The Maker's Name. Doran, Carol and Thomas H. Troeger. New York: Oxford University Press, 1986.
- A Star Not Mapped On Human Charts (23)

Presbyterian Hymnal, The. Editors. Louisville, KY: Westminster/John Knox Press, 1990.
- As With Gladness Men Of Old (63)
- Brightest And Best Of The Stars Of The Morning (67)
- Bring We The Frankincense Of Our Love (62)
- From A Distant Home (64)
- Midnight Stars Make Bright The Sky (65)
- O Morning Star, How Fair And Bright
- What Star Is This With Beams So Bright (68)

Psalter Hymnal. Brink, Emily, Editor. Grand Rapids, MI: CRC Publications, 1988.
- Bright And Glorious Is The Sky (360)
- Christ Is The King And He Shall Reign (359)
- How Bright Appears The Morning Star (357)
- O Son Of God The Father (368)
- Songs Of Thankfulness And Praise (361)

Second Avery And Marsh Songbook. Avery, Richard and Donald Marsh. Carol Stream, IL: Agape, 1983.
- Morning Star, The (35)

Sing To God: Songs And Hymns For Christian Education. Hawkes, Mary and Paul Hamill. New York: United Church Press, 1988.
- I Wonder As I Wander (71)
- Little Baby Jesus (77)
- Now The Kings Are Coming (88)
- O Come, Little Children (76)
- Once For Us A Boy Was Born (79)
- This Highway, Beheld At Break Of Day (87)
- To Jesus From The Ends Of Earth (85)

Songs For All Seasons. Avery, Richard and Donald Marsh. Carol Stream, IL: Agape, 1984.
- Follow The Star (17)
- Without A Star To Follow (5)

Songs Of Hope And Peace. Illinois Chapter United Church Of Christ Fellowship In The Arts. New York: Pilgrim Press, 1988.
- As We Journey Toward Bethlehem (45)

United Methodist Hymnal, The. Editors. Nashville: United Methodist Publishing House, 1989.
- Angels From The Realms Of Glory (220 - Verse 3)
- Christ Is The World's Light (188)
- Christ, Whose Glory Fills The Sky (173)

- Epiphany (255)
- First Noel, The (245)
- I Want To Walk As A Child Of The Light (206)
- O Splendor Of God's Glory Bright (679)
- On This Day Earth Shall Ring (248 - Verse 3)
- Silent Night, Holy Night (239 - Verses 3, 4)
- Sing We Now Of Christmas (237 - Verses 4, 5)
- There's A Song In The Air (249)
- We Three Kings (254)
- We Would See Jesus (256)

Spend an entire church school class singing Epiphany songs. Invite individual classes to learn a hymn and to present an Epiphany concert for the congregation and community.

SHINING STARS

PURPOSE

To add the rays of a star to a banner as illustrations of ways in which God's love extends to many people. It will help the children review the wonderful way in which God guided the Wise Men to the Christ child.

PREPARATION

You will need the following materials for this activity:
- Fabric for background
- Material for rays
- Sewing machine
- Thread
- Permanent markers
- Fabric glue
- Dowel rod or pole
- Cord
- Polyester stuffing material

In preparation, cut the fabric for the banner background to the desired size and shape. Since the liturgical color for the season of Epiphany is green, this would be a good color to use for this piece. Seam the sides, if necessary. Sew a casing for a rod across the top of the banner.

Cut a star shape approximately one-third the size of the banner background. Use bright, shiny material such as lame, taffeta or satin to create the star. Position the star in the upper portion of the banner and sew it in place. Stuffing may be added behind the star to give it a three dimensional effect.

PROCEDURE

The brilliance of a star shining in the sky led the Magi to the location of Jesus, the Light of the world. In this project, the symbol of the star is used on a banner as a way to help the children review the wonderful way in which God guided the Wise Men to the Christ child. The activity will also enable the children to remember that at the time of the visit of the Wise Men, God revealed Jesus as the one who would bring salvation to all people. Most importantly, this learning opportunity will encourage the children to respond to the fact that many people in the world are still in darkness and do not know the love of Jesus. By adding rays to the star on the banner, each person will be invited to share the love of God in a special way.

As the children arrive, show them the banner. Ask what is missing on it. The answer is rays. Rays illustrate light reaching to many places. Remind the group that a star led the Wise Men to the place where Jesus and his family were staying. This can be done by telling the Bible story, Matthew 2:1-12, with flannelgraph, listening to a recording of it, or acting it out in a dramatic form. Invite the children to explain what it means when the Bible says that Jesus is the Light of the World. Tell the class that Epiphany is an important time because it is when God revealed that Jesus, the Light, would bring salvation to all people.

Each person who believes in Jesus is like a ray which extends Jesus' light and love to many places. Brainstorm ways in which this happens. Ideas include being kind to a new person in the class, sharing food or clothes with people who need them, and asking someone to a special activity at church. Invite each child to add a ray to the banner. At the time the ray is put into place, a special prayer will be offered.

Provide a variety of bright, shiny fabrics and allow each person to select a piece. Help the individuals cut rays of different shapes and sizes. Names may be written on the pieces with permanent markers.

Assist the participants as they take turns gluing the rays to the banner background. The rays may also be added with a sewing material which is an iron-on fusible bonding. As each child attaches his or her piece, offer a prayer, using the person's name, and thank God for the many ways in which the love of Jesus can be spread by this individual.

Insert the rod into the casing at the top of the banner. Attach cord to each end of the pole and hang the banner in a prominent place in the classroom or in the church building. Encourage each child to tell one person who will view the banner about the meaning of the project.

GLOW-IN-THE-DARK GALAXY

PURPOSE

To make glow-in-the-dark stars to use in imagining what it would have been like to be led by a specific star.

PREPARATION

You will need the following materials for this activity:
- Posterboard, white
- Star patterns, many sizes
- Circle patterns, various sizes
- Poster paint, glow-in-the-dark florescent
- Ultraviolet light bulb(s) (place in several light fixtures)
- String, various lengths
- Masking tape
- Brushes
- Cans or plastic tubs
- Water
- Pencils
- Scissors
- Paper punches

PROCEDURE

Help the children make glow-in-the-dark stars and use them to imagine what it would have been like to have been one of the Wise Men.

Distribute star and circle patterns, together with posterboard, pencils and scissors. Tell the young people to trace and cut a variety of stars and circles out of the heavy paper. Remind each person to make one star larger than the rest to represent the star of the Magi.

Provide glow-in-the-dark florescent paint, brushes and clean-up materials, and assist the children as they design and decorate the shapes.

Prepare the pieces for hanging by using the paper punch and punching a hole into each design. Pass out string of various lengths and tell the children to thread one piece through the hole in each star and circle. Tape the strings with the designs to the ceiling.

Invite each person to imagine being one of the Wise Men who followed the special star which led to the Christ child. Turn on the ultraviolet light and encourage the children to enjoy the beauty of the glow-in-the-dark galaxy. Read Matthew 2:1-12 to the group as they star gaze.

Remind the children that reading the Bible on a regular basis is one way to discern God's leading and direction in their lives.

SCRIPTURE STARS

PURPOSE

To review Scripture passages which refer to Jesus as the light and to record them on star mobiles to give as special gifts.

PREPARATION

You will need the following materials for this activity:
- Construction paper
- Pattern for six pointed star (page 29)
- Scissors
- Yarn or string
- Markers
- Bibles
- Lists of Scripture passages

PROCEDURE

The symbol most often associated with the story of the Wise Men is the star. Its light led these earthly kings to the location of the Lord of heaven and earth. There are many scripture passages which speak of Jesus as the light of the world. Some are: Isaiah 60:1-6, John 1:1-14, John 8:12, John 9:5, John 12:46, I Peter 2:9 and Revelation 22:16. Help the children become familiar with some of them by using the "Scripture Stars" activity.

Distribute a Bible and a Scripture passage list to each student or small group of participants. Invite them to look up the verses and to read them silently, and then, in turn, aloud to the whole class. Discuss the various ways in which these verses refer to Jesus as the light.

Invite the children to record and remember some of these verses in a special way. Show them how to make an Austrian star. Select two different colors of construction paper. Using the pattern provided, cut a six pointed star from each piece. Make a slit to the center from the top of one star and to the bottom of the other. Provide supplies and assist the children as they prepare these pieces.

Help each participant pick a "light" verse to write on his or her star. Hand out markers and tell them to write the verse on the left half of one star and the biblical reference on the right half of the other. Slip one star over the other.

Make a hole in the top of each star, thread yarn or string through it and hang the stars throughout the room.

Give the stars as special gifts to people who have modeled that Jesus is the light of their lives or someone who needs to know of Jesus' light.

SIX-POINTED STAR

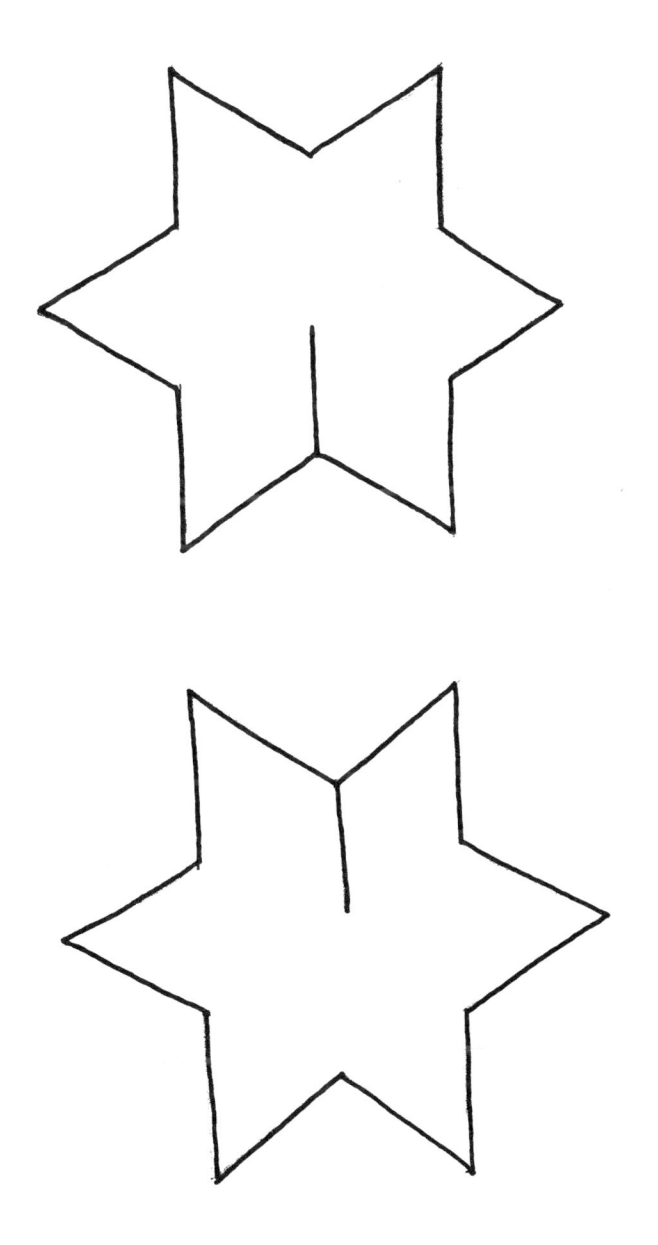

29

Faithful Followers

PURPOSE

To use paper stars as a method for setting and attaining goals for following Jesus in our lives.

PREPARATION

You will need the following materials for this activity:
- Star patterns (page 31)
- Paper
- Construction paper, yellow
- Scissors
- Pens or pencils

PROCEDURE

The Magi had a goal: to find the Savior. To accomplish this purpose they followed the star that God sent to lead them on their journey. Teach the participants to be star followers and help them set goals for ways in which they can follow Jesus in their own lives.

Begin by brainstorming a list of ways in which the children follow Jesus. After the group has identified several ideas, distribute a piece of paper and a pen or pencil to each person. Invite the young people to write down several personal goals for following Jesus at home, church and school. These could include writing a letter to a forgotten friend, spending 10 minutes in quiet prayer, or baking something and sharing it with classmates.

Pass out yellow construction paper, scissors and star patterns. Tell the children to cut out several star shapes and to write or draw a goal on each of them. Allow the group to make as many stars as time and interest permits. The more stars that are made, the more stars that will be followed.

Tell the boys and girls to take the stars home and to hide them throughout the house to be found and followed during the year.

STAR PATTERNS

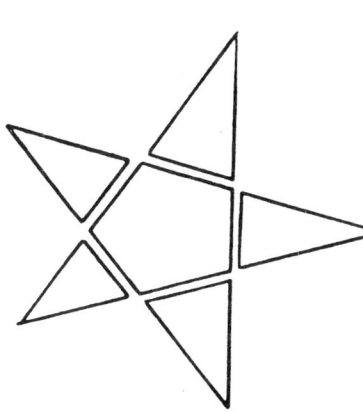

SEARCHING FOR THE SAVIOR

SYMBOL: PATH

OVERVIEW

The search for the Savior took the Wise Men down many paths. Leaving their homeland in the Middle East, probably Persia, they most likely followed the course of the Euphrates River past Babylon and then started southward along a main trade route into Jerusalem. By going this way they would have had water, food and lodging during their travels. The trip certainly brought them into many types of terrains: mountains, deserts, lowlands and river valleys. They passed through the countries currently called Iran, Iraq, Syria, Jordan and Israel.

For the most part, the places the Wise Men went, the people they met and the stories they shared are unknown. It is recorded that their journey took them to the palace of King Herod where they inquired of the location of the newborn King of the Jews. Upon hearing it to be Bethlehem, they continued their trip and were led five to seven miles further down a road which took them to this city. At the place where the star rested, the Magi entered the house where the infant and his family were staying, and worshiped the Savior.

Because the men were warned by God in a dream of Herod's wicked plans to destroy the infant, they went home by another route.

The activities in the section "Searching For The Savior: Path" will help the participants recall the events which happened in the process of the Magi's journey as well as assist them in reconstructing, recounting and recording paths in their own lives which lead them closer to Christ.

Seeker's Story

PURPOSE

To use a choral reading to tell the story of the journey of the Magi.

PREPARATION

You will need the following materials for this activity:
- Copies of Seeker's Story Choral Reading
- Cassette tape of music without words
- Tape player

PROCEDURE

Proclaim the Epiphany story by using the dramatic, poetic method of choral reading. Invite four people to read the parts, and allow time for them to practice the words and phrases. When the reading begins, play soft music in the background to help set the mood.

SEEKER'S STORY

One: Once, many, many years ago, in a land far away, there lived three kings,
Two: Melchior,
Three: Gaspar,
Four: Balthasar.
One: These kings spent their lives studying the stars. Each night they watched the sky and the stars.
Two: They would write down all they learned.
Three: They would write where they thought the stars came from,
Four: And where they were going.
One: One night, a bright and beautiful star appeared in the sky.
Three: Each of the kings looked into the old books
Two: And found that the new star was a sign that a great king was to be born.
Four: So each king left his home to follow the star,
One: The star that would lead them to the infant-king
Two: To honor and worship him.
Three: And each carried a gift.

Four: Melchior took gold;
One: Gaspar carried frankincense;
Two: Balthasar brought myrrh.
Three: After days and days of travel,
Two: They came near to Jerusalem.
Four: The star disappeared
One: And they didn't know what to do.
Two: "Let us ask King Herod,"
Three: "Yes, Herod will know of the birth of another great king."
Four: "Where is the one who has been born king of the Jews?"
One: "We have seen the star."
Two: "We have come to honor him."
Three: Herod was a wicked man.
Four: He was angry at the visit of the kings
One: And their news of a greater king than himself.
Two: He went to his chief priests and asked about this child.
Four: "It has been written: a king is to be born in Bethlehem."
Three: "Go to Bethlehem and find out all that you can about this infant-king."
One: The kings set out once again for Bethlehem, not knowing that Herod wanted to kill the infant-king.
Two: There in the sky, they once again saw the star.
Three: They followed it
Four: Until at once it stopped over the place
One: Where the child was born.
Two: Like flames of wild fire dancing in the sky
Three: The star pointed to Jesus,
Four: The King of Kings.
One: They went in and saw the infant with Mary, his mother.
Two: They fell on their knees and gave him honor.
Three: They opened their treasures
Four: And offered the gifts
One: Of gold,
Two: And frankincense,
Three: And myrrh.
One: That night in a dream, the kings were warned of Herod's wish to destroy the child. So they returned to their countries by a different way.

Use this choral reading during an Epiphany worship service or as part of the lesson for a church school class. A family could share the reading before having a special epiphany dinner.

DIORAMA DISPLAY

PURPOSE

To construct dioramas depicting scenes of the journey of the Magi and discuss ways the children search and find Jesus in their own lives.

PREPARATION

You will need the following materials for this activity:
- Shoe boxes
- Paint
- Paintbrushes
- Construction paper
- Glue
- Scissors
- Markers
- Clothespins, old-fashioned wooden ones
- Pipe cleaners or chenille wires
- Fabric scraps
- Yarn or fake fur

PROCEDURE

The Wise Men must have traveled a great distance to find the Savior. Recreate one or many parts of their journey by constructing individual or group dioramas. Each child may make his or her own shoebox scene or one may be built by the whole class in a large cardboard carton.

Review the story with the learners and help each person decide which part of it to depict. Some ideas would be: the place in which the Magi studied the stars, a town through which they passed, or King Herod's court in which questions were exchanged.

Invite each child to select a box to use. Tell the group to set it on its side, so that the bottom of the box becomes the back of the scene. Point out the supplies: paint, paintbrushes, construction paper, glue, scissors and markers. Show the children how to cover the outside of the box with paint or paper. Also demonstrate how to create the background of the scene on the inside of the box. Assist the young people as they complete this part of the project.

Refocus the group's attention and illustrate how to make figures of the Wise Men and other characters by using pipe cleaners and/or clothespins. Add fabric scraps for clothes. Camels and other animals may be made from this technique as well. Have the children set the completed pieces inside their boxes.

As the children finish their projects, talk with each person about ways he or she searches and finds Jesus in his or her own life.

Display the dioramas and invite other church school classes and members of the congregation to view them.

SCRIPTURE SEARCH

PURPOSE

To work a word search game containing various parts of the story of the Magi's journey.

PREPARATION

You will need the following materials for this activity:
- Copies of the Word Search game
- Pencils

PROCEDURE

The Magi searched to find the Savior. Use the Word Search game to help the children identify various parts of the story.

Read Matthew 2:1-12 to the group. Pass out a game sheet and a pencil to each person. Allow time for the children to complete the activity. Review and clarify any part of the story, as needed.

Encourage the children to make up other games based on this Scripture passage. This could include crossword puzzles, mazes and scrambled words.

Find the following words in the word search game:

MAGI	STAR
JESUS	SAVIOR
LIGHT	SEARCH
WISEMEN	KINGS
HEROD	EPIPHANY
GOLD	FRANKINCENSE
MYRRH	BALTHASAR
CASPAR	

```
M G G V A X T O C A I M R A P S A C K O
F O H L W M R K O W Z G S I H J P L U I
E V Y E Y T G I D L O G F Z Z O M M D Q
S H Z P S I P G G H V Q U S K S I O T U
N B E W H N K L P A C U Z D F X N X B O
E I C R M B Y Z P B M F D C S E I L K I
C M I U O R A S A H T L A B B N S R N M
N G P H R D T G I S H H S I L U S W K O
I Z A A Q W M K R Z G S S E E W U Y N F
K J T L V E E X A M K S U F A P S J W R
N S G J U R J T R K F D P C S R W T A T
A M E L C H I O R P S W B E L M C R H E
R U B U Z F M K T N T U P F Y R N H I V
F W I S E M E N A A A I S R Z T G F K G
M Y K S J P Z A D C P H R E K M K S O W
I F I I R O T X I H P H V D J J R A Z G
M D N P X W Y M A G K T H G I L Z V O J
D B G E T J P N A P Y H F M A Q H I E H
R T S A Z H Y G I S R B B A B E N O Q X
M H Z S L L Y V P K Z O Q Q J R Q R Q A
```

PERSONAL PATHS

PURPOSE

To reflect on paths that are traveled throughout life and to record experiences that occur on them.

PREPARATION

You will need the following materials for this activity:
- Construction paper
- Crayons or markers
- Pencils
- Scissors
- Hole punch
- Yarn

PROCEDURE

The kings traveled many roads to find the Redeeming One. They journeyed long and hard on a route that was unfamiliar to them. Led by a star, they followed several paths in the hope of finding the infant Jesus so that they could worship him and pay him homage. With God's guidance, the kings even traveled another road to return home.

The "Personal Paths" activity offers an opportunity for the participants to reflect on and to write about paths that they have traveled and are traveling in their lives. Begin by asking the children to think for a minute or two about places they have visited that bring them good memories. These places can be near or far; across the ocean or right next door. Ask the group to reflect on some of the following things:

- What feelings are associated with each place?
- What is special about the place?
- What was experienced there?
- What was learned by taking that path?
- Was it a new experience?
- If the path is a familiar, frequently taken road, what new discoveries have been made along it?

Tell the learners that they will have the opportunity to record, remember and own the experiences by creating a book of foot-shaped stories and drawings. This can be an individual or a group project. Each person may make his or her own book, or one book may be compiled by the whole class.

Invite each person to choose several pieces of construction paper. State that one sheet will be needed for each experience that is to be recorded. Tell the group to trace one of their feet on each sheet of paper and to cut it out. Make crayons or markers available and instruct the children to write a story or a poem or to draw an illustration or a picture of one of their "paths" on each foot.

When each child, or the whole class, has a collection of feet, punch a hole in one end of each paper. Use a piece of yarn to bind the sheets together to form one or more books.

Gather the group in a circle and invite those who wish to share their experiences to take a turn to do it. Remind the children to travel familiar paths with a sense of anticipation and expectation of discovering new things, and to venture out on new journeys with the assurance that God is guiding them.

FAITH-FILLED FOLLOWERS

PURPOSE

To use modeling clay to shape symbols of paths people take to find Jesus. This will help the children identify ways in which they seek to find Jesus in their own lives.

PREPARATION

You will need the following materials for this activity:
- Paper
- Pencils
- Modeling clay, non-hardening
- Background music
- Audio equipment

PROCEDURE

Women and men, shepherds and kings, boys and girls came to see the baby Jesus. Both the very poor and the very rich traveled to honor the King of Kings. Men who rode camels and women and children who walked on foot adored the child the prophets had predicted. Some people came in sandals while others would have worn soft slippers made of the finest materials. Perhaps the shepherds wore sandals or no shoes at all. All these people, from different walks of life, came to the same place on varied paths.

This simple clay activity is designed to help the children explore the paths that they are taking as they search for the same King. Begin by brainstorming ways in which people today find Jesus in their day to day living. Ask the group questions, such as:

- What are some of the paths that lead you to Jesus?
- Do you ever have to go out of your way to find Jesus?
- Do the paths and choices you make help or hinder finding Jesus?

As the brainstorming takes place, ask the learners to name feelings that are associated with the sharings. These may be written down, too.

When the discussion subsides, give each person a piece of modeling clay. Invite the group to mold a shape or a feeling associated with one or more of the ideas and issues that were mentioned. Soft background music may be played as the group works.

Invite the participants to share their sculptures and to talk about the many places that their paths lead them to find Jesus.

SYNCOPATED STORY

PURPOSE

To tell the story of the Wise Men's journey in a rhythmic way that will help the children to remember the event.

PREPARATION

In advance, you should practice the story to establish the pattern of the beat.

PROCEDURE

Tell the story of the Wise Men's visit to Jesus by clapping a rhythm and echoing a rhyme. In a "Syncopated Story" the leader says a line, and the participants repeat it back. Begin by establishing the clapping pattern, one clap on the knees and one clap of the hands, and practice it several times. Chant the first line of the story to this rhythm and tell the group to echo it back. Communicate the entire message in this manner. Maintain the established rhythm throughout the activity.

Three Wise Men went on a journey.
They had to travel very far.
They passed through deserts and mountains,
And were guided by God's star.

They arrived at the palace of Herod.
He was ruler of the land.
They asked where to find the baby.
It was all part of God's plan.

Herod called his chief priests together
To determine where the babe might be.
Bethlehem was the answer they gave him.
The Wise Men would go and see.

When the Magi left King Herod
The star shone very bright.
It led them to the Savior
It was a holy night.

The Wise Men gave their treasures
To honor the newborn king.
All earth and heaven would join them
Jesus' glory and greatness to sing.

SYMBOLS OF THE SAVIOR

SYMBOL: GIFTS

OVERVIEW

The gifts that the Wise Men gave to the Christ child were significant for several reasons. They were the fulfillment of Old Testament prophecies, they provided information about the Wise Men and the area from which they came, and they described the person and work of Jesus.

Psalm 72:10,11,15 prophesied that kings from Sheba and Seba would bring Jesus gifts, specifically gold. Isaiah 60:6 adds that incense will be offered as well.

The gifts also indicate that the Wise Men came from the Middle East. The Persians made a ritual of bearing a gift whenever they saluted their kings. These people offered valuable presents to show their subjection to a person of distinction. Gold, frankincense and myrrh were some of the most valuable products produced in this region, and therefore illustrate the country of origin of the travelers.

Most importantly, the treasures foretold that Jesus was to be the King of Kings, the perfect High Priest and the Savior of the world. Gold, a precious metal often given to kings, was presented to the Holy One by the Wise Men. It signified Jesus' kingly rule over all nations. Frankincense, a white resin which gives off a sweet fragrance when burned, symbolized Jesus' high priestly role. It was used in the temple during worship and sacrifices to God. Jesus, fulfilling the role of a priest, made it possible for people to enter the very presence of God. Myrrh showed that Jesus had come into the world to die. It was an aromatic gum resin, obtained from a tree, that was used to embalm the bodies of the dead. Sometimes myrrh was mixed with wine to form a drink. This was the mixture given to the Savior when he uttered the words, "I Thirst" during the crucifixion.

"Symbols of the Savior: Gifts" contains six activities that will help the participants affirm their own God-given gifts and those of other people. The learning experiences will also encourage the children to show gratitude to God for His special gift, Jesus, by reaching out to others.

Clothing Collection

PURPOSE

To decorate cardboard cartons to symbolize the Wise Men's gifts and to use the boxes to facilitate a children's clothing collection.

PREPARATION

In advance, obtain permission to leave the containers in locations in the church and the community. Contact agencies that will distribute the clothing to needy people.

You will need the following materials for this activity:
- Cardboard cartons, three
- Paint
- Brushes
- Clean up materials
- Foil wrapping paper
- Trims
- Scissors
- Glue
- Paper
- Markers
- Pens

PROCEDURE

Explain that this project involves two parts. The first consists of decorating three large cardboard boxes to symbolize the containers of gold, frankincense and myrrh that the Wise Men gave to the infant king. The second part entails collecting clothing for young children and offering it to agencies that provide services to people in need.

Supply paint, brushes, clean-up materials, foil wrapping paper, trims, scissors and glue. Challenge the children to make the cartons look like there is something of value inside them. Divide the participants into three groups and invite each team to decorate a box. When the boxes are completed, and the art supplies are put away, place the containers in a prominent location in the church or in the community.

Ask the participants to bring or collect new and used clothing for infants and young children. Encourage them to involve others in the congregation in the project.

Make posters and display them in the church and in the community. Write announcements to include in the church bulletin or newsletter or in a local newspaper.

When the boxes are full, deliver them to agencies that will distribute the clothing to people with infants and young children. Possibilities would include missions, homeless centers, or refugee resettlement programs.

PURPOSEFUL POETRY

PURPOSE

To use creative writing as a method for exploring ways in which the gift of love can be shared with others.

PREPARATION

You will need the following materials for this activity:
- Construction paper, red
- Paper
- Pens or pencils
- Scissors

PROCEDURE

The Wise Men offered Jesus gifts of gold, frankincense and myrrh. These costly treasures represented the Magi's great respect and adoration for the Christ child. Each person has many gifts to offer the Savior as expressions of his or her love and gratitude to him. The most important one is described in a beautiful poem written many years ago by Christina Rosetti. Share it with the group and have them respond to its message by writing a poem describing a way in which they show their love for Jesus.

What can I give him,
Poor as I am?
If I were a shepherd,
I would bring a lamb.
If I were a wise man,
I would do my part.
Yet, what can I give him?
I'll give him my heart.

Invite the children to reflect on the words of the poem. Guide them in discussing what they can give to Jesus. What gifts do they use to share the words and stories of Jesus with others?

The heart is a symbol of love. Jesus, the most perfect example of love, asks his followers to love others as he loved them. Writing poetry is a creative way for people to express the love in their hearts and in their lives. Writing is also a method to encourage the learners to look at the gifts that have been given to them and to consider how they use these gifts to honor Jesus.

Distribute pieces of paper and pens or pencils and ask the children to write a simple four line poem describing a way in which they show love for Jesus. An example might be:

The love I have in my heart
Is a gift I hold so dear.
I give it to my neighbor
To show that Jesus is here.

When the children have completed this process, pass out sheets of red construction paper and scissors. Ask each person to cut his or her paper into the shape of a large heart. As much of the full sheet should be used as possible. Tell the participants to copy their poems onto the heart.

Take turns having the class show and share their poems. Submit the creative writing projects to the church newsletter or make a bulletin board display with them.

GREAT GIFTS

PURPOSE

To name and affirm the gifts of other people as a means of helping the children discover the gifts that people bring to each other's lives.

PREPARATION

You will need the following materials for this activity:
- Paper
- Pencils

PROCEDURE

Ask the children to name some of the Christmas gifts that they received from friends and family. After items such as games, toys and clothes have been mentioned, tell the children that there are other gifts people give to them every day. Suggest some gifts that people bring to each other's lives, such as laughter, encouragement and patience.

Arrange the learners in groups of two's and instruct the participants to take turns naming and affirming the gifts of the other person. It may be helpful to provide paper and pencils so that a list can be made. Challenge the young people to come up with a gift for each letter of the alphabet. For example, A — affirmation, B — belief, and C — confidence.

Conclude with a time of prayer in which each participant thanks God for the gifts of the other person.

Tangible Treasures

PURPOSE

To share treasures with special people and relate the experience to the Wise Men bringing gifts to the Christ child.

PREPARATION

Invite the children to bring a treasure to the next class or meeting. It should be something that is important to them and that they are willing to give to a special family member or friend. Recommend that the participants go through their special things at home. Explain that a treasure is something that a person holds dear; something that is very significant and important. It might be a book or record, a picture or postcard, a doll or a toy. Suggest that the learners recall the person who gave the item to them and the circumstances surrounding the event. Recommend that the young people try to identify one or more reasons why the item is important. Ask each person to pick one treasure that he or she could give as a gift to a loved one or friend, and to bring it to the next session.

You will need the following materials for this activity:
- Special treasures brought by the participants
- Stationery
- Envelopes
- Pens
- Boxes
- Wrapping paper
- Scissors
- Tape
- Ribbon

PROCEDURE

Upon arriving at the place where Jesus, Mary and Joseph were staying, the Wise Men presented the infant Savior with treasures from their homeland. The gifts symbolically described the person and work of Jesus. Gold, indicating royalty, symbolized Jesus' rule over all nations. Frankincense, a sweet smelling incense, represented prayers rising before God and symbolized Jesus' high priestly role between men and women and God. Myrrh, an oil used at the time of burial, pointed to the fact that Jesus would die for the sins of humankind.

Gather the children and invite them to show the treasures that they have brought to class. Encourage each person to share the reason that the item is important to him or her. Take time to talk about the people who will be receiving these gifts. Be sure each participant has identified a person to whom the treasure will be given.

Like the Wise Men, have the children prepare to present their packages. Allow each learner to pick a box, to put the gift inside it, and to wrap it attractively.

Make a variety of stationery and note cards available and instruct each person to take a piece to use for the activity. The children will also need pens or pencils. Tell them to use the stationery paper and to write a note to the special friend telling that person how important he or she is and why the gift is being given. Remind the group to write about the Wise Men and the gifts that they brought to Jesus. Provide envelopes and have the children attach the letters to their gifts.

Take time to pray with the children before they leave. Thank God for the wonderful gift of Jesus, and for the gift of a special person in each child's life. Pray that the gifts may be given and received in a spirit of love.

TREE TRIMMING

PURPOSE

To use a Christmas tree in a way that will provide gifts for the birds.

PREPARATION

You will need the following materials for this activity:
- Christmas tree, undecorated
- Popcorn, popped
- Cranberries
- Thread or string
- Needles
- Scissors
- Pine cones
- Peanut butter
- Seed
- Containers
- Oranges
- Suet
- Knives
- Newspapers

PROCEDURE

January 6, Epiphany, is a day on which many households take down the Christmas decorations. Instead of discarding the tree, use it in a way that will offer gifts to the birds.

Tell the children that a Christmas tree will be placed outside and invite them to make the birds edible decorations to place on it.

Show the young people how to make garland by stringing popcorn and cranberries onto thread. Provide directions for creating additional decorations such as pine cones dipped in peanut butter and seed, orange slices, and pieces of suet. Allow time and encourage the children to cooperate to make a variety of items.

Bring the tree outside and trim it with the new decorations.

Another tradition involves using the trunk of the Christmas tree to form a cross which is used in a worship center during Lent and Easter. Dry out the tree. Trim off the branches and discard them. Cut the trunk into two pieces, of varying lengths, and fasten them together to form a cross. Use it as a focal point of worship during Lent. Trim it with lilies on Easter Sunday.

REFLECTIVE RESPONSES

PURPOSE

To journal on the gifts the Wise Men brought to Jesus and the gifts people have in their own lives.

PREPARATION

You will need the following materials for this activity:
- Journals or paper
- Pens or pencils

PROCEDURE

The Wise Men came to worship the infant Jesus. In their hands they carried gifts from their own country which they presented to the King of Kings. These gifts were symbolic in their giving. Gold, a precious gift given to kings and queens, is a true symbol of royalty. Frankincense, a fragrant resin people burned when they prayed to God, symbolized Jesus' high priestly role. Myrrh, a special perfume often used to prepare a body for burial, represented that Jesus came to die.

This creative writing activity is intended to enable the children to reflect on the gifts that the Wise Men brought to the Christ child and to consider special gifts in their own lives.

After reviewing the Epiphany story, and emphasizing the gifts that the Wise Men brought to Jesus, invite the children to respond to each gift by writing about it. Give each person a piece of paper or a journal and a pen or pencil. Suggest that the children write their thoughts, reflections or prayers in response to the following statements and questions.

Gold

Gold is a rare and precious gift given to kings and queens. When the Wise Men gave it to Jesus, it symbolized that he was the king of heaven and earth. What gift in your life is most precious to you? What do you hold very dear? What do you need to let go of in order to let God in?

Frankincense

Frankincense is a sign of prayer and celebration. It symbolizes prayers rising before God and the posture of prayer with arms outstretched to God. What do you want to celebrate in your life? Who do you want to celebrate? What do you long for? What do you pray for?

Myrrh

Myrrh, a precious perfume, is an oil that functioned as a preservative. In Jesus' time, it was used to prepare a body for burial. What memories in your life do you save? What do you cherish and preserve?

Gifts

What special gifts do you have? How do you use these gifts? How are these gifts sacred?

When the group has finished journaling, invite anyone who wishes to share thoughts, reflections or prayers to do so before the participants are dismissed.

SURRENDER TO THE SAVIOR

SYMBOL: HANDS

OVERVIEW

The English word "worship" has been said to derive from the word "worth." When one worships God, that person is praising God for His great worth. When the Wise Men found the Christ child, they worshiped him. In their custom, and in the manner in which homage was paid to earthly kings in that time, they fell prostrate before him. The Magi demonstrated their adoration with their whole beings as well as with their gifts. This action indicated that they acknowledged that Jesus was greater than the Magi and that they were subject to his authority.

Six activities are included in the section "Surrender To The Savior" and are intended to encourage the participants to worship Jesus, the King of Kings and the Light of the World.

PRAYERFUL PROCESSION

PURPOSE

To participate in a service in which the rooms of a home or a church are blessed as one of the special customs celebrated on Epiphany.

PREPARATION

You will need the following materials for this activity:
- Candles
- Matches
- Incense
- Incense container
- Cross
- Gifts or symbolic gifts
- Container of water
- Evergreen branch
- Chalk

PROCEDURE

Among the special customs celebrated on Epiphany is one of blessing the rooms of a home or church and imploring God's protection in the coming year. Invite the children to participate in this ritual.

Organize the event by deciding the order in which the rooms will be blessed and which person will offer the prayer in each place. Show the children the items that will be used on the journey. These include candles, which may be lit or unlit, incense, a cross, symbolic gifts, water and an evergreen branch. Invite each child to choose something to carry on the walk.

Process through each room. Sing, if desired. Bless each room by saying things like:

In The Kitchen: May this kitchen be a place of nourishment for our relationships as well as for our bodies.

In the Church Office: May this room be a place for doing God's work in our world.

In The Classroom: May this classroom be a place of listening to and learning more about God.

Use the evergreen branch to sprinkle water around the space.

Chalk the frame of the front door as a symbol of welcome and hospitality. The initials of the traditional names of the three Wise Men, Gasper, Melchior and Balthasar, are used together with the year's date. Crosses between each letter and number implore God's protection in the year ahead. For example, the chalkmark should look like this:

19 + G + M + B + 92.

Conclude with a prayer surrendering the space to God and thanking God for the assurance of safekeeping through the coming year.

Invite families or the entire congregation to participate in the service.

CREATING WITH CLAY

PURPOSE

To use clay in a worship experience to illustrate ways in which people participate in building the kingdom of God.

PREPARATION

You will need the following materials for this activity:
- Clay, self-hardening
- Tape of instrumental music
- Tape player

PROCEDURE

God sent Jesus to heal the whole of humanity. Jesus is the Incarnate Word, the Redeemer, the Savior, the Messiah. His journey and course in life took him beyond the cradle to the cross where life won over the power of death for all people. When Jesus walked the earth he touched the lives of the people around him in many ways. He reached down to raise up a sinner, he embraced the leper, and he touched the blind and gave them sight.

The only hands Jesus has today are the hands of those who believe, like those of the shepherds, kings and later the apostles. People must use their hands to help build the Kingdom. All Christian people are called to this challenge. The clay hands activity will help show the importance of everyone's contribution in touching the lives of persons around them.

Gather the participants together in a circle. Turn on soft instrumental music. Set a lump of clay in the center of the group. Pray the following prayer or another appropriate prayer:

Creator God,
You fashioned humanity out of clay and water. Help us today to use the creative gifts that You have given to us to shape, mold and build the kingdom here on earth. Allow our work to touch the lives of all people. We ask this in the name of Jesus because we believe. Amen.

Invite the participants, one at a time, to shape, mold, bend or form the lump of clay, giving no specific directions for the outcome. After everyone has had a chance to touch, work, add to or shape the piece, conclude with a spontaneous prayer. Remind the participants how different the piece of clay became because of the touch and care of each hand.

MEDITATIVE MOMENTS

PURPOSE

To reflect on the use of hands as instruments to worship Jesus and to build God's kingdom.

PREPARATION

You will need the following materials for this activity:
- Background music
- Cassette, record or CD player
- Art or writing supplies

PROCEDURE

Guided imagery is a creative method to use to help people experience a situation. Although today's children did not participate in the Wise Men's visit to the infant Jesus, they can use their imaginations to envision the awe and wonder of that event. Use this meditation and quiet time to enable the learners to reflect on the importance of worshiping Jesus with their hearts, their hands and their whole bodies. This experience will also encourage the group to ponder ways to use their lives in the service of others.

Gather the group and ask each person to assume a comfortable position. Tell the people to become aware of their own heart beats and breathing patterns. Invite the participants to sit still and to reflect on God's love.

Put on soft background music without words. Begin to read the meditation.

Guided Meditation

Close your eyes and in your mind picture your own hands. What do they look like? How big or how small are they? Do you like what your hands look like?

Imagine your hand holding the hand of a small baby. Look at the little fingers. Feel how soft the hand is. See how big your hand is as it is wrapped around the baby's hand. Hold that tiny, soft hand for a moment and thank God for the gift of this new life.

Now, in your mind's eye, imagine your hand in the hand of another person whom you have met on your life's journey. The person could be a child, teen, young adult, middle aged man or woman or a senior citizen. Look at the fingers. Are they bent or a bit uneven? Are the hands soft or rough? How do they look next to yours? What can you tell about this person by looking at his or her hands?

Think for a moment about the last time you offered a hand to help someone. God gave us hands as instruments to use in surrender and service to Him. God gave us hands to use in building the kingdom. How do you use your hands to build the kingdom?

Picture in your mind Jesus, many years after the Magi's visit, reaching his hands out to you. See his hands wrapped around yours. Notice the nail marks. What do they look like? How does it feel to be holding the hands of Jesus? These are the hands that were nailed for you. These are the hands that raised Lazarus, cured the leper, healed the blind, comforted the prostitute, and offered bread and wine to his disciples as his body and blood. Look at the face of Jesus. Look into his eyes, and in your heart of hearts say whatever it is that you want to say to Jesus. Spend time in each other's comfort and presence.

When you are ready, open your eyes and come back to this room.

Following the guided meditation, provide an opportunity for the participants to express their feelings about the experience. This can be done in several creative ways. Make the necessary supplies available and spend time journaling, painting, developing gestural interpretations or writing poetry or prose. Those who wish to may share their reflections with the entire group.

SPECIAL SYMBOLS

PURPOSE

To discuss ways in which hands are used in worship and to create peace symbols from hands.

PREPARATION

You will need the following materials for this activity:
- Construction paper, white
- Doilies
- Pencils
- Scissors
- Markers, black
- Glue
- Paper clips, thread, yarn or string

PROCEDURE

The Magi came to worship the Prince of Peace. In their hands they carried treasures which they offered to the newborn King as an act of worship.

Begin by asking the children to name ways in which people today use their hands to worship Jesus. A pastor types a sermon, an artist paints a picture and a composer writes a song. More specifically, invite the young people to name ways in which they use their hands to worship God. Some may play musical instruments, others might use sign language to interpret for the deaf, and a few could write poetry.

Distribute a sheet of white construction paper, a pencil and scissors to each participant. Tell the children to trace one of their hands onto the paper. Remark that each hand will be turned into a dove, a symbol often associated with peace. Show the group how to cut out the hand so that the thumb is turned into the head of the bird. Provide time for the children to cut out their hands. Make markers available and demonstrate how to make a dot on each side of the head to represent eyes. Small pieces of white doilies may be glued near the finger area, or wings, to add texture and detail to the doves.

An opened paper clip or a piece of thread, yarn or string may be added to the top of the dove to serve as a hanger for the piece.

Spend time talking with the children about ways in which their hands can be use to promote peacemaking in worship and in other situations.

Litany Of Light

PURPOSE

To worship God for the ways in which Jesus has been born anew in each person during Advent, Christmas and Epiphany.

PREPARATION

Prepare a worship center in one area of the church school classroom. Place the Bible, candles, matches and incense stick on the table. Set a tape and tape player up in this area.

You will need the following materials for this activity:
- Candles, six
- Matches
- Bible
- Incense stick
- Cassette tape or CD of instrumental music
- Tape or CD player
- Table

PROCEDURE

Christmas has come and gone. Epiphany Sunday has been celebrated. Decorations in the church and the classroom have been packed away for another year. The environment has changed, and so have the people who have participated in the events of these special seasons. Christ has been born again in each heart and life. This simple worship service will help the participants to savor the meaning and memories of experiences that are now a part of their lives.

Guide the participants to the worship center. Invite the group to sit comfortably together. Play reflective music softly in the background and call the children to quiet prayer.

Read the Christmas and Epiphany stories from the Bible. The Christmas story is found in Luke 2 and the Epiphany passage is contained in Matthew 2. Discuss the readings and talk about special events that occurred in the life of each person during these seasons. Emphasize ways in which lives have been changed during this time of the year. Ask how each person is different than he or she was before Advent,

Christmas and Epiphany began. How has God been born within them? How have they grown?

After the sharing, read the following litany together. The response after each statement is: "Lord of Light, Hear Our Prayer." Practice the phrase as a group before beginning the reading. Light a candle after each response. Burn the incense before the beginning of the litany.

Litany

God, giver of all blessings, grace our hearts with the gift of Jesus' love.
LORD OF LIGHT, HEAR OUR PRAYER.
Creator Lord, healer of the broken, renew our world.
LORD OF LIGHT, HEAR OUR PRAYER.
Help us Holy One, to never put away or to forget the goodness of our memories. Help us to share them with others.
LORD OF LIGHT, HEAR OUR PRAYER.
Giver of Peace, continue to spread peace to all of humanity.
LORD OF LIGHT, HEAR OUR PRAYER.
Source of light and wisdom, lead us out of darkness, make us wise on our journeys.
LORD OF LIGHT, HEAR OUR PRAYER.
God, we ask your blessing in the name of Jesus who is the Messiah.
LORD OF LIGHT, HEAR OUR PRAYER. AMEN.

After the litany, sit quietly. Gently encourage the children to enjoy the sound of the music, the light of the candles and the fragrance of the incense as they savor their own memories of Advent, Christmas and Epiphany. After an appropriate interval, dismiss the children.

SIGNING A SONG

PURPOSE

To learn sign language for a song as a way of using hands to praise God.

PREPARATION

Arrange for someone to accompany the singing.

You will need the following materials for this activity:
- Music, "O God, We Adore You"
- Accompaniment

PROCEDURE

Help the children learn to praise God with their hands as well as their voices. Teach the participants the song, "O God, We Adore You." After they are familiar with the words and the music, help them learn sign language to accompany each verse. The signs are:

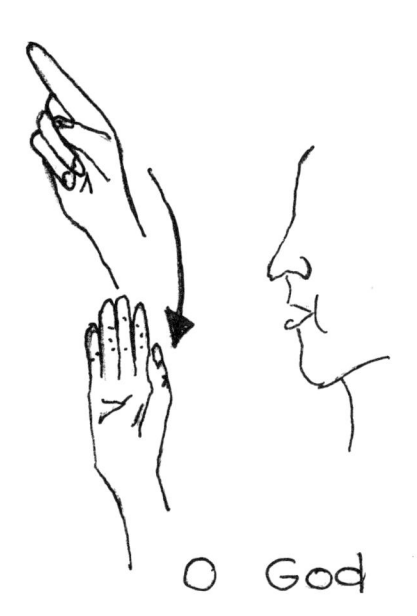

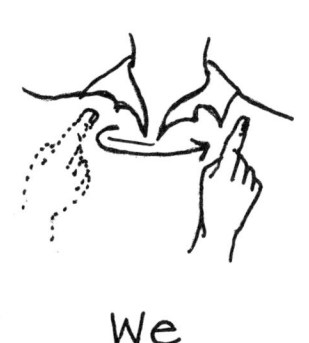

O God

We

68

adore You.

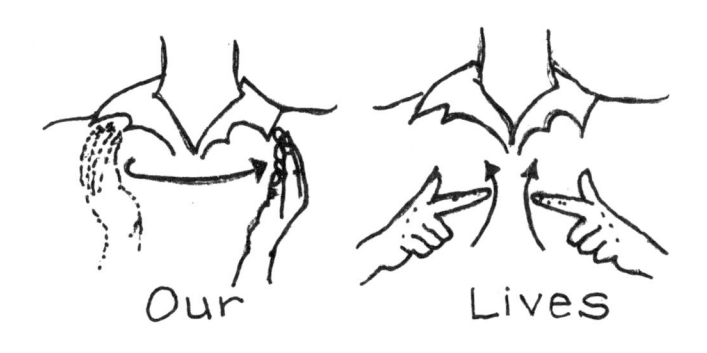

Lay Our Lives

Before You.

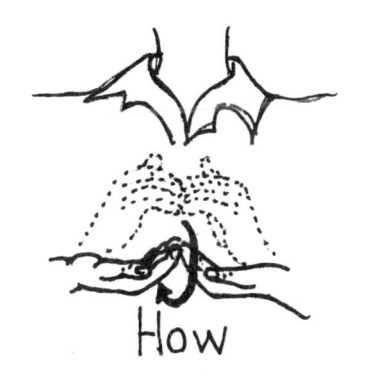

How  We

Love or You.

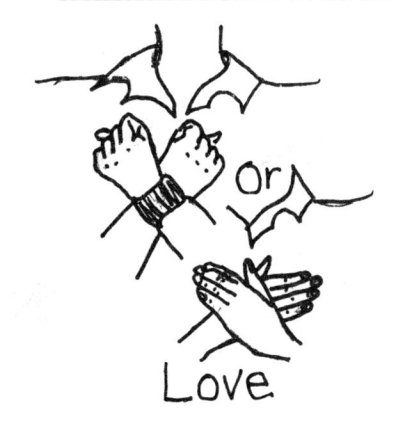

Jesus

Spirit

The right palm is above and facing the left palm with fingers spread; as the right hand moves up, the index and thumbtips of both hands close.

Sing and sign the song during children's worship or church school. Invite the young people to provide special music for an Epiphany service or a social event. Small groups of children may visit the shut-ins of the church and share the message with them.

SERVING THROUGH THE SAVIOR

SYMBOL: WORLD

Overview

During Epiphany, Christians celebrate the manifestation, or coming, of God to all people in Jesus Christ. The Old Testament book of Isaiah contains many prophecies regarding the nations coming to the light of the Lord (Isaiah 2:2, 11:10, 51:4, 56:7, 60:3, 66:18).

The Wise Men were led by a star to seek and to find the Light of the World. The Magi symbolically represented the coming of all nations to the light of Jesus. Jesus' salvation is for the whole world.

The goal of the six activities for the theme "Serving The Savior" is to provide creative and caring ways in which the participants may spread the message of the Gospel to people of the world, both near and far.

PATCHWORK PIECES

PURPOSE

To make a paper quilt depicting ways to share the Good News of the Gospel with people around the world.

PREPARATION

Pre-cut butcher paper or newsprint to the desired size. This will serve as the background for the quilt. Individual squares, made by each child, will be glued to it. Prepare a grid on the butcher paper for the construction paper patches. Measure one square onto the paper for each person participating in the project. For example, if there are 16 children in the class, measure an equal number of squares onto the background. One-half of a sheet of construction paper, 4 1/2" X 6", is a good size for each square. Leave at least three inches between the squares and around the outside edge of the butcher paper to serve as a border. Cut construction paper into 4 1/2" X 6" pieces. Arrange for audio-visual materials and/or a speaker on local and world mission projects. Obtain equipment for the audio-visual presentation.

You will need the following materials for this activity:
- Butcher paper or newsprint
- Yardstick
- Pencils
- Construction paper
- Magazines
- Markers
- Glue
- Tacks

PROCEDURE

Epiphany is the time in the church year to move from the story of the birth of Jesus to the proclamation of the Good News that a Savior has come for all people. There are many ways in which children can share this message with others. During the "Patchwork Pieces" activity, participants will discover things that they can do to spread the Gospel. Through involvement in a group project, making a paper quilt, each person will decide on one way in which he or she will tell someone else about God's love.

Review the story of the Magi found in Matthew 2:1-12 with the class. Remind the children that Epiphany is a time when God revealed that Jesus was to be the Savior of the world. Ask the group to name ways in which this Good News is being shared with people near and far. Provide pictures, slides or videos of local and world mission projects. If arrangements have been made for a speaker, invite the guest to make a presentation.

Help the children focus on ways in which they can spread the news of God's love. Discuss ideas such as serving at a soup kitchen, visiting a homebound person, reading a bible story to a young child or giving an offering to support a missionary. Tell the children that they will have the opportunity to depict one of the ideas by making a square that will be placed on a patchwork quilt.

Various techniques can be used to illustrate the ideas. Try having the children draw pictures with markers or crayons or create collages by cutting pictures from magazines and gluing them to the squares. Distribute the pre-cut construction paper squares, markers, crayons, magazines, scissors and glue. Allow time for the group to complete their pictures. Circulate through the room as the children work, and encourage each person to live out his or her commitment.

When the pictures are finished, help the children glue them to the grid on the background paper. Invite the children to complete the border of the quilt by adding designs such as crowns, stars, crosses, or worlds. These may be drawn on with marker or cut out of construction paper scraps and glued into place.

Tack the completed project to a wall in the classroom or display it in an area of the church where other people may view it. Refer to the quilt during the season of Epiphany and invite the children to share ways in which they have lived out their commitments to spread God's love.

New Narratives

PURPOSE

To write and tell a cooperative story based on the Epiphany experience as a fun way for children to share their understanding.

PREPARATION

You will need the following materials for this activity:
- Pen or pencil
- Paper
- Cassette tape, blank
- Tape player

PROCEDURE

Imagine the tales that were told by the shepherds and the Magi after visiting the infant Jesus. They would have shared stories of a Messiah King lying in a manger of straw, among the farm animals of the cave. There could have been accounts of a young mother holding, loving and cradling God's son to her heart. Years later Jesus taught in stories. He told parables as he walked the countryside and met with the people. Stories were a medium the people could understand and through it he communicated the love of God to them.

This creative writing and storytelling activity is included to provide a fun way for a class to share their understanding of the Epiphany story and to expand the narrative to include ways in which this message is being shared with people around the world.

Ask the participants to sit in a circle on the floor. Select one person to be the storywriter and give him or her paper and a pen or pencil. This person may participate in telling along with writing. Choose one person in the circle to begin the activity.

Ask the children to recall the events of the Epiphany story silently. Explain that the class will cooperate to tell the story in a special way. Each person, in turn, will say one word which will add to the narrative that is developing. Each word as it is said should be written down in succession by the recorder. Depending on the number of people involved, indicate how many turns each participant will take. The story may develop something like this:

There.....was.....a.....star.....that.....was.....seen.....by.....Wise Men.....in.....a.....country.....far.....away.....

After the story is told and written down, choose a reader with a clear voice to record it with background music. Play the tape back for the whole group to hear.

Once the account of the Epiphany experience is completed, ask the children to try the process again. This time record a story of ways in which this message is reaching to people around the world. This may include examples from nearby and far away.

Share the stories with other church school classes or make several copies and deliver them to home-bound church members.

PROJECTING PEOPLE

PURPOSE

To participate in a media project focusing on the variety of people for whom Jesus came into the world.

PREPARATION

In advance, make arrangements for a class field trip.

You will need the following materials for this activity:
- Camera
- Slide film or photo film
- Slide projector or poster board
- Glue
- Tape of quiet music
- Tape player

PROCEDURE

As an infant, Jesus was visited by many people. The travelers came from all walks of life. Poor shepherds who worked in the fields, women on their way to market, children going to play among the hills, and wise travelers bearing riches and wealth all came to pay homage to the Christ child.

Jesus was born to save all people from sin. He was given to all people so that a broken world could be made whole. Jesus came for people of all races and nationalities. His love extends to all humanity. Use this media project as a wonderful way to help the children see the richness of people of all ages and backgrounds. Reflect on how all people are connected because of the Redeemer, Jesus.

Plan a class trip to a large inter-cultural city. Spend a day visiting different ethnic neighborhoods and learning more about various cultures. Tell the people in each area that the group is working on a media project for a church school program. Ask permission to take some pictures. Photos of a wide variety of men, women and children, both young and old, would serve the project best.

After the pictures are developed, make posters of the photos to illustrate the fellowship of all people, saved by the love of Jesus. Or, put an audio-visual meditation together using the slides that were taken, and write a simple script set to soft music.

Offer a time when the program can be presented to other groups and organizations in the church. Celebrate that the Savior the Wise Men sought at Epiphany came for all people.

WORLD WALK

PURPOSE

To use movement and music to celebrate that the message of Epiphany is for all people of the world.

PREPARATION

Cut sheets into strips 3/4" wide and 4 to 5 feet long. One strip is needed per participant. Fill a bucket with sand or rocks and position a pole in the center of it.

You will need the following materials for this activity:
- White sheets
- Scissors
- Pole from broom, rake or dowel
- Nails or tacks
- Hammer
- Bucket
- Sand or rocks
- World map
- Encyclopedias and reference books

PROCEDURE

Epiphany is a time to celebrate that Jesus came to bring salvation for people in every nation. This activity will give the young people an opportunity to participate in praising God for this Good News. Invite each child to select a country of the world. Refer the boys and girls to the map and to the encyclopedias and reference books. Allow time for the children to find the flag of their particular country. Tell them to note its colors and design.

Distribute one fabric strip to each child. Make permanent markers available. Have the group decorate the fabric strips with the colors of the flags of their nations. Tell the children to write the name of the country on the end of the strip.

Help the children nail or tack the other end of the strip to the top of the pole. All pieces of fabric will be hanging down. Suggest that the children look at the different strips and become familiar with the countries they represent. Explain that Epiphany is a time to celebrate that the Gospel belongs to all the people of the world.

Instruct each person to take the free end of a strip and to walk around the pole while singing. A good song to use is Avery and Marsh's "The Great Parade." (Avery, Richard and Donald Marsh. Carol Stream, IL: Hope Publishing Company, N.D.) The strips will wind as the children walk. Reverse the direction so the fabric can unwind.

Use the pole in an intergenerational or community Epiphany celebration.

SINGING SONGS

PURPOSE

To sing songs which express God's love for the world.

PREPARATION

In advance, arrange for an accompanist for the singing. Locate equipment to play the recordings.

You will need the following materials for this activity:

- Music to songs such as:
- "He's Got The Whole World In His Hands"
- "It's A Small World"
- "We Are The World"
- "What The World Needs Now"
- "Love In Any Language"
- "For God So Loved The World"
- Accompaniment
- Equipment such as record, cassette or CD player

PROCEDURE

During the season of Epiphany, people celebrate the manifestation, or coming of God, to all people in Jesus Christ. Jesus reinstated this mission in the words of the Great Commission, Matthew 28:18-20.

There are many songs associated with a world theme. Share some of them with the participants. Hold an Epiphany sing-a-long during a portion of the class, or play the music on records, tapes or CDs.

Choose a familiar tune and ask the children to write new words to it on an Epiphany theme. For example, using the tune "Row, Row, Row," the new words could be:

Jesus came to bring God's love
To people everywhere.
In our homes, at school and church
We need to show God's care.

PARTICIPATORY PRAYERS

PURPOSE

To use the song "Jesus Loves The Little Children" as a directed prayer for the people of the world.

PREPARATION

You will need the following materials for this activity:
- Music, "Jesus Loves The Little Children"
- World map
- Address of denominational world mission board
- Paper
- Pens
- Envelopes
- Stamps

PROCEDURE

"Jesus Loves The Little Children" is a familiar song which emphasizes the message of Epiphany that Jesus came to bring salvation to all the people of the world. It can be sung with the children and also used to lead them in a guided or directed prayer.

Ask the group to sing the first verse together. Invite them to participate in a prayer in which they can remember children in all parts of the world. Sing the first two lines of the song again. Stop after the phrase "All the children of the world." Explain that the seven continents will be named and that a brief pause will follow each statement. Encourage the group to pray for the people of that particular region during the silence. Suggest that they remember their physical and spiritual needs.

Name each continent, Africa, Antarctica, Asia, Australia, Europe, North America and South America, and pause briefly after each of them. After the prayer, sing the remainder of the song and conclude with "Amen."[5]

Invite each child to select a country and to write to the denominational world mission board for information on ways in which the Gospel is being proclaimed in that location.

[5] Wezeman, Phyllis Vos and Jude Dennis Fournier. Fifty Ways For The Fifty Days. Brea, CA: Educational Ministries, Inc., 1990, p. 41. Adapted with permission.

BIBLIOGRAPHY

Barclay, William. The Gospel Of Matthew, Volume 1. Philadelphia: Westminster Press, 1975.

Barnes, Albert. Notes On The New Testament: Matthew And Mark. Grand Rapids, MI: Baker Book House, 1956.

Daniel, Rebecca, Compiler. Biblical Christmas Performances: Plays, Poems, Choral Readings, Stories and Songs. Carthage, IL: Shining Star Publications, 1988.

Daniel, Rebecca, Compiler. Biblical Christmas Plays And Musicals: Plays, Musicals, Songs, Skits And Tableaux. Carthage, IL: Shining Star Publications, 1989.

Editors. About Epiphany. South Deerfield, MA: Channing L. Bete Company, Inc., 1989.

Esther, James R. "Service Planning: The Season Of Epiphany." Reformed Worship. Grand Rapids, MI: CRC Publications, Fall, 1987, p. 41-43.

Hart, Dirk J. "Revealing The Glory Of God." Reformed Worship. Grand Rapids, MI: CRC Publications, Fall, 1989, p. 40-43.

Heideman, Eugene P. "Reaching Out Or Drawing In?" Reformed Worship. Grand Rapids, MI: CRC Publications, Fall, 1989, p. 38-39.

Hickman, Hoyt L., Don E. Saliers, Laurence Hull Stookey and James F. White. Handbook Of The Christian Year. Nashville: Abingdon Press, 1990.

Lee, Sharon. A Rainbow Of Seasons: A Leader's Resource For Living The Church Year. Minneapolis, MN: Augsburg, 1983.

Mathson, Patricia. Burlap & Butterflies: 101 Religious Education Activities For Christian Holidays. Notre Dame, IN: Ave Maria Press, 1987.

Mathson, Patricia. Pray & Play: 28 Prayer Services and Activities For Children in K Through Sixth Grade. Notre Dame, IN: Ave Maria Press, 1989.

Schneider, Kent and Sr. Adelaide Ortegel, S.P. The Burst Of Christmas: Alternative Christmas Celebrations. West Lafayette, IN: Center For Contemporary Celebration, 1975.

Simcoe, Mary Ann, Editor. A Christmas Sourcebook. Chicago: Liturgy Training Publications, 1984.

Tasker, R. V. G. <u>The Gospel According To St. Matthew: An Introduction And Commentary</u>. Grand Rapids, MI: Eerdmans, 1968.

Torrance, David W. and Thomas F., Editors. <u>Calvin's Commentaries: A Harmony Of The Gospels Matthew, Mark and Luke, Volume 1</u>. Grand Rapids, MI: Eerdmans, 1975.

Wildeman, James. "Epiphany: What Do We Celebrate?" <u>Reformed Worship</u>. Grand Rapids, MI: CRC Publications, Fall, 1987. p. 2-3.

CREATIVE IDEAS FOR ADVENT
Volume 1

*edited by
Robert G. Davidson*

Every church should have one or more copies of this book from which the staff and lay leaders can gather ideas to implement during the holiday season. A wealth of suggestions for special programs, displays, family activities, and more have been collected in this resource.

This creative planning aid is conveniently divided into three sections—All Church Activities, Children's Activities, and Youth Activities. None of the material, however, has to be limited to only one area of programming. Material can be drawn together from any of the three sections to best benefit your needs.

Item: 2516 $12.95
ISBN 0-940754-06-1

CREATIVE IDEAS FOR ADVENT
Volume 2

*edited by Robert and
Linda Davidson*

If you have used **Creative Ideas for Advent,** you will be excited to learn of its sequel, **Volume 2**. This is another valuable resource that every church staff should have to participate fully in the joy and celebration of the Advent season.

This creative planning aid is conveniently divided into four major sections—All Church Activities, Children's Activities, Youth Activities, and Family Activities. In its pages you will find Advent wreath services, children's Christmas stories, activity projects, service projects, meditations, lesson plans, puzzles, games, plays, and a host of other resource articles that will provide a new approach to traditional Christmas festivities.

Item: 2526 $12.95
ISBN 0-940754-35-5

CREATIVE IDEAS FOR ADVENT
Volume 3

*edited by
Linda S. Davidson*

Due to the popularity of our Creative Ideas For... series, we have collected another volume for Advent. Again it is divided into four sections: All Church Activities, Children's Activities, Youth Activities and Family Activities. Included in this volume are: family celebration suggestions, Advent wreath services, stories, meditations, craft ideas, service projects, worship services and more.

This resource will help you plan more meaningful activities for the Advent season. We preach the Good News of Jesus Christ over and over, but often fear it is falling on deaf ears. Here you will find activities to make the real meaning of the season come alive in your church. This collection of all-new material will enhance your congregation's Advent season by making the message of Jesus Christ come alive.

Don't miss this exciting volume of Advent ideas. Start planning now for Advent as you think about an all-church Advent workshop, or a project which will reach out to touch your congregation and bring them joy during this special season of the year.

Item: 2536 $12.95
ISBN 1-877871-00-1

CREATIVE IDEAS FOR LENT
Volume 1

*edited by
Robert G. Davidson*

After the successful response to **Creative Ideas for Advent,** we now offer a similar fine resource for Lent. In its more than one hundred pages, this book includes intergenerational events, worship ideas, activity projects, youth programs, lesson plans, stories, and many other ideas for use during the Lenten season.

The material is divided into three major sections—All Church Activities, Children's Activities, and Youth Activities. This does not mean that any of the material has to be limited to certain age groups. The possibilities are infinite of how you can use the ideas in this book.

Item: 2521 $12.95
ISBN 0-940754-25-8

CREATIVE IDEAS FOR LENT
Volume 2

*edited by Robert and
Linda Davidson*

Due to the popularity of **Creative Ideas for Lent,** we have edited another seasonal resource. Here you will find more materials to make your Lenten programs truly memorable.

Included in this volume you will find several plays, worship services, intergenerational events, crafts for children, study program ideas, meditations, puzzles and quizzes, youth programs, and much more.

In addition to the three regular sections—All Church Activities, Children's Activities, and Youth Activities—we have added a new one, Family Activities. We hope people will find material here to make the Easter event more meaningful to each member of the family.

Item: 2531 $12.95
ISBN 0-940754-62-2

Order from:

EDUCATIONAL MINISTRIES

1-800-221-0910